Pannerselvam Dharmalingam is an avid reader of current affairs and is particularly interested in forces – philosophy, history, economics, politics, culture, language, geography that had shaped humanity and continues to do so. Writing poems is one way for him to share his thoughts with the world that he hopes would lead to more nuanced interactions across the globe.

Dedicated to my late father Gopal Dharmalingam

Pannerselvam Dharmalingam

MY EARTHLY REFLECTIONS

AUSTIN MACAULEY PUBLISHERS™

LONDON • CAMBRIDGE • NEW YORK • SHARJAH

A CIP catalogue record for this title is available from the British Library.

ISBN 9781398443600 (Paperback)
ISBN 9781398443617 (ePub e-book)

www.austinmacauley.co.uk

First Published 2024
Austin Macauley Publishers Ltd®
1 Canada Square
Canary Wharf
London
E14 5AA

This book would not have been possible without the encouragement and love of my wife, Valli and daughter, Nithilla. More than anyone, they kept motivating me to pen my thoughts and look for publication opportunities. Special thanks to my loving sister, Wasugi, for her constant guidance and love throughout my life even if she had settled in the Netherlands for the last three decades. Special gratitude is also due to my mother and sisters in Singapore for their love and patience throughout my life. Finally, I owe a debt of gratitude to Austin Macauley Publishers for their faith in my work and publishing it.

Table of Contents

A Woman for All Seasons

A woman for all seasons all my life
That's you, only you.

You are the autumnal lips
That dances to the rhythm of the breeze
Like the trees paying homage to the arrival of autumn by
Flooding the earth with their leaves,
Only upon seeing you will my soul be at peace.

So protective are you of me
Of the coming winter when life will be bleak and empty,
That you descent from heaven to earth to be with me.

Winter is sadness
Winter is darkness
Winter is lonely
But you enliven me with your embrace that is so heavenly.

Spring brings to the forefront your flourishing blooms
To clear the receding winter gloom.
A gloom when I always momentarily lose my sight

Only for you to move me away from the canopy of winter
white
To regain my sight
To enjoy the hue of colours
That the earth offers.

Life returns to earth in spring
Lights and colours return to ecstasy on brink
And you are unfailingly there, with a smile on brim
Year after year, spring after spring.

Spring earth gently drowns in colours
And once again, our spring romance begins in earnest
In preparation for our summer love.

Summer comes
And summer love returns
When you make me loved, the affection my heart always
yearns
Year after year, summer after summer.

Summer returns me to the zenith of my life
To the zenith of love
The zenith that is you
My Angel, My Lover, My confidant.

Summer heat wands its magic on all meadows
Summer affirms my deep love for you that never mellows.

Autumn, winter, spring, summer
White, grey, blue, red, yellow, orange

Sadness, darkness, gay
They do not matter to me
As long you are with me.

The angel of my life
The lover of life
The confidant of my life
The Woman for All Seasons, you are my life.

A Time for Everything

Time waits for no one
Know when to embrace it
And have the foresight to know when to let go of it.

There is a time to love
There is a time to say goodbye!

There is a time to dream
There is a time when dreams become reality
If they don't, there comes a time to say goodbye!

There is a time for kiss
There is a time to give the kisses a miss
Know the difference, and love will never cease.

There is a time to pursue puppy love
There is a time to make passionate love
From puppy to passionate, intimacy grows with verve.

There is a time to laugh
There is a time to cry
Make time for them to grow closer to each other.

There is a time for ecstasy
There is a time for despondency
Without them, a fulfilling life can never be.

There is a time to be active
There is a time to be passive
Know the difference, and the wiser, you will be.

There is a time to embrace your children
There is a time when the embrace can become suffocation
Know when to let go of the embrace
Nothing in life is eternally the same.

There is a time to work
There is a time to rest
Practice it and your soul will suffer less.

There is a time for family
There is a time for friends
They make for a more fulfilling life that never ends.

There is a time to agree
There is a time to disagree
Have the wisdom to make space for this reality.

There is a time for winning
There is a time for losing
The courage to acknowledge this makes for less suffering.

There is a time for ideals
There is a time for reality
They are part of life's totality.

There is time to learn
There is a time to teach
Learning and teaching are the perfect antidotes to ignorance.

Time waits for no one
Time goes marching on,
Whether you like it or not.

Time is Life
Life is Time
Make time to put your life in order
Make time for everything for a fulfilling life.

A Smile

Smile…Your smile is such a mystery to me
So intoxicating and charming, it will always be.

God must have smiled when she first saw you
For such a smile can only be exquisite on a beautiful face
Like you.

It is such a mystery to me
Your smile heaves from heaven with glee.

Mystics and even angels may travel the world to look for
Saints to worship.
But in you, I see the one smile that helps to build kinship
Keep smiling for a beautiful world to be…

All Alone

My journey in loneliness
A heart filled with emptiness
I seek forgiveness
Instead, I only face smallness.

Yes! the smallness of human forgiveness.

But, who can I blame, but myself!

The depth of my shallowness
The breath of my wickedness
I now understand the lack of forgiveness.

I am all alone, all alone!
Nowhere to go, but to my empty home.

Once, I dreamt of immortality.

I was on a mission
Everything was to precision
Anything that was intermission faced disqualification.

No room for laughter, or time to banter
No soft nerves for tears and laughter.

Iron was in my blood
In my heart and soul, power, not compassion, was in flood.

I worshipped fortune
I loved the attention, that was but opportune
I craved for power.

I had no qualms on its destructive notes of sour
But now, I have become half-a-man.

I have fortune
But I now realise that I am not immune.

Immune to companionship, love, and, family.

I am now alone, all alone!

Once, I disdained love for family life
Now, I long for one.

I now realise how fleeting and superfluous the attention to
be
People wanted money, not my personality.

And, when they all had their fill
I was treated as a run-of-the-mill.

I now cry alone, all alone!
I now understand why I am alone
For, I had turned cold, in my heart and soul.

I saw human life only as a linear progression
One way forward, no turning to the sides, or, back for
transmission.

I failed to see the many opportunities for happiness.

Happiness in love, and, in sadness,
Happiness in sharing wealth,
Happiness in forgiveness,
Happiness in imperfections.

Once, I worshipped only money and power
I did not comprehend the need for gentle touches of a true
lover.

I now crave for a loving hug,
I now want a shoulder to cry on,
I want someone to wipe away my tears of loneliness.

Where are the hugs, where are the shoulders?
Come to me, come to me!
I am alone, all alone.

Once, I dismissed people's need for family and love as
weakness
Now, I realise how wrong I have been
And how small was I in my humaneness.

Yes, I have succeeded beyond my wildest dreams
But those dreams had no place for warmth, sincerity, and,
sharing.

I destroyed many lives with my thirst for power, fame, and,
money
Now, I want to make up, but no one wants to listen to me.

Saint voices warned me long ago
But I dismissed them as no hopers as born losers
Now, I crave for them
But they are not to be seen.

Now, I yearn for the simplicities of life:
Simplicity of love,
Simplicity of laughter,
Simplicity of pleasure.

But in the absence of anyone to share with, I am all alone
I want to turn a new leaf in my life
But, sadly, there is no one to walk with me.

I am all alone, all alone!

Beauty

Your eyes…They are a sight to behold
For in them, I see the angel of my life unfold.

Smile…Your smile is every poet's dream of the perfect
beauty
Hoping, hoping that it stays that way forever
For, a more perfect beauty, he will never discover.

Voice…Your voice brings cheers when I am down,
Hope when I am in despair, and smile when I am in tears
For, without it, I will crumble in my fears.

Poise…Your beautiful poise breezes with touch gentle
And, it ravages my world as a sweet angel.

Laughter…Your laughter charms me to no end
It makes me hope it will never end.

Love…Your love is heaven on earth
For, you are GOD's answer to earth's quest for beauty and
love
God created you with the angel's sense of beauty,

A saint's capacity for unremitted love,
A child's sense of innocence,
And, a mother's ability to sooth wounded hearts.

Your beautiful flame will forever be…

An Angel of Colours

Oh Athena, Goddess of Wisdom
Listen to me, Listen to me, please, please, please?
I met an Angel of a woman, an Angel of Colours
Her name is Nadiya.

She is the violet of my soul
Who can calm my heart with spiritual mastery that I behold!

Yes, Yes, me! Can you believe it?
A man given to revulsion, not compassion
A man given to resentment, not redemption.

And here, this angel mysteriously walks into my life
And changes me for afterlife.

Oh Selena, Goddess of the Moon
Listen to me, Listen to me, please, please, please?

Nadiya is my Angel
In whose blues I have found my youth
Eternal truth
Sincere love.

Yes, Yes, me! Can you believe it?
A man only used to violence and dissension
A man only given to hatred, not love mansion.

Oh Hera, Wife of Zeus and Goddess of the Moon
Listen to me, Listen to me, please, please, please?

Nadiya in who's red I found passion, confidence, courage.

Yes, Yes, me! Can you believe it?
A man only used to pessimism, not optimism
A man only given to brute courage, not moral courage
O Helen of Troy, daughter of Zeus
Listen to me, Listen to me, please, please, please?

Nadiya in whose orange I found warmth, vitality, creative
love.

But, Nadiya is more, so much more
I have simply run out of lexicons to describe her.

She is as pink as a calming and joyous love,
She is as yellow as a wise and happy love,
She is as white as a pure and clean love.

And, and, she is still so much more
Please, please…continue to listen to me!

Her poetry can turn a rock into a gemstone
And, the words from her lips are as sweet as honey
To my starving soul:

We are Mark Anthony and Cleopatra,
We are Romeo and Juliet,
We are Tristan and Isolde.

Oh Athena, Selena, Hera, Helen
Bless my Angel of Colours, Nadiya.

Be a Hero

If you want a world where everyone lives with dignity,
purpose and love
Then, start with yourself and the world will follow your
actions with verve.

Try it!

If you want a world where people accept one another's
diversity
Then, you must first move away from your adversity
It is the only way to move up the chain of humanity.

Believe in it!

If you want the world to love you
Then, you need to start loving people without any hue.

Practice it!

If you want a world that is paradise kingdom
Then, live by the scriptures of peace, tolerance and wisdom
That is the only way to build up a new fiefdom.

Do it!

If you want to empower humanity
Then, start empowerment in your inner sanctity
Where, often-times, wives, sisters, mothers, and daughters
live in oblivion
Empower them to be equal partners for a world free of
suffering silence.

Free from the silent suffering from misogyny.
Free from the silent suffering from flesh trade.
Free from the silent suffering from human trafficking.
Free from the silent suffering from child labour.
Only then, dreams and aspiration can women harbour.

Do it!

If you want generations to enjoy the richness of mother earth
Start now by speaking up against environmental degradation
Only then, can we leave a worthy legacy to future generation

Practice it!

Never regret being born into this world
It is a unique gift to be part of a magical evolution.

We have heroes of many types
Women and Men,
Big and small,
White, yellow, and black,
Christians, Muslims, Hindus, Buddhists…the list goes on.

Be a Rachel Beckwith who died at age nine
But who had started giving at age five
To make a difference in other children's lives.

What a Heroine!

Be a Nujood Ali,
Married at age ten to a man three times her age
Determined she was to be free
She went all out and won and free she will ever be.

What a Heroine!

Two pint-sized heroines
What difference they have both made to humanity
So much to teach us about honour, beliefs, bravery.

Is it not our time to be Heroes too?

Eternal Kiss

The ring on your nose, the shimmering pearl of eternity
The luscious eyes, the citadel of beauty
The smile of yours that brings a poet to kneel for tender
Mercy.

The epitome of your total beauty
The spice that adds to your eternal flame of love
That anyone feels when you gently breeze by them
Is your kiss.

You kiss me so passionately that my world is suspended on
thin air
So suspended that when you stop, my soul always despairs.

Your kiss makes me cry
A cry of passion and triumph for reaching the zenith of my
life
To be kissed by you,
The angel of my life,
The paragon of human life,
Is to reach my eternal guide.

In your kiss, I find my life renewed
Where there was once despair, I now find hope
Where there were desolate terrains in my dreams of
yesterday
I find vivacious colours today.

Where the world pours scorn on my looks
Your kiss showers me with virtuous love
A love with a child's sense of innocence
A love with a mother's ability to sooth wounded hearts
A love that is a drop of honey to my barren life
That I will always cherish until I die.

Your kiss lets streams of passion flow through my veins
It is a kiss of art that sets all other kisses apart.

Kiss me until I collapse into your arms
For in your arms, I feel renewed hope
You are my citadel of love, purity, beauty.

Kiss me for me to stay alive forever.

I reach for the sky to touch the angels to give my thanks
I climb up to reach the doorsteps of planet moon to give my
thanks
For giving me you, who loves me for who I am.

With you, my faith in humanity, in GOD is renewed
Kiss me, kiss me
But am I in a dream world?
I opened my eyes in fear that it may be so.

But there, in your eyes, images of our kiss appeared
And the pearl of your nose smiled,
As if to say, "Don't fear, I am still here."

Yes, I am in the real world, caressed by the woman of my
life
Oh, what glory for me, today, every day
The kiss by this angel that has drowned my doubts forever
And in its place, gave birth to a whole new self
Full of love, confidence, cheers.

Your kiss is a kiss of liberation
Liberty from crushing resentments
Self-doubts and disappointments.

Oh, what glory now I feel for my life!

Your kiss suspends all lives on earth momentarily
When, even angels of love fly down to know the cause
Only to cover their faces in embarrassment
For never having witnessed such a kiss even in heaven.

Your kiss is rhythmic
It rhymes with my heartbeat.

Your kiss is so gentle, so loving
That it chases away all my heartaches, fears,
And helps renew my soul anew.

When you kiss
Your eyes sparkle even as my heart trembles
It caresses my fears into hope.

Your kiss gives me life,
Your kiss adds spice to your body, to my life,
Your bountiful bosoms, your robustly titillating belly,
Your tantalising neck,
Your everything comes alive with your kiss.

Your kiss with me is the spice of my life
The eternal kiss of my life.

Eyes

Once I dreamt of my beauty
My beauty for a partner, for a wife, for a Goddess.

I chose the path to the kingdom of Venus
The Goddess of Beauty.

Such a beauty only exists in paradise, people told me
But I refused to believe such sanctimonies
In my heart and mind, I fervently asked Venus not to fail
me.

And then, I saw your eyes
Eyes like no others
Eyes of Venus
Mesmerised was I, and, all thoughts of life beyond you
became hopeless.

When your luscious eyes wand their magic spell, I turn into
a statue
And, speechless I become, as if on cue.

Your eyes…Your eyes
There is so much to wonder
In their presence, my heart flutters.

Your eyes…Your eyes
Their quixotic beauty makes my emotions go wild.

In your absence, my soul takes leave of my body and goes
away,
In search of the sanctity of your eyes, so strong is their sway.

Come, seat next to me
For, I cannot get enough of your eyes.

Talk to me with your eyes
Kiss me with your eyes
Embrace me with your eyes.

Your eyes …Your eyes
When they sparkle, rivers turn into streams of honey
Nectar becomes aplenty
Life flourishes, and, earth blossoms once again in ageless
beauty
And, dreams of better days kept alive in perfect harmony.

Oh, luscious eyes!
Your smile eyes transform the chattering voices of the sky
into rhapsodic
The perfect complement to our love that is harmonic.

Quixotic, Rhapsodic, Harmonic
They are your eyes
And, your eyes are so much more
Come, keep me company for a more complete love ever to
be.

Drenched in Passion

Immersed in unremitting ecstasy
Passion was the lifeline to us
Without it, we would have fallen apart.

Lust filled our bodies to the brim
It drowned my fear
And, I became a slave to her.

A slave to her dominant lips, hands, breasts that explored all
my body
Lips oozing streams of honey wherever she kissed
Flesh that tickled at her fingertip touches
My lips lusted for her ample breasts
So soft, so smooth, I kissed them slowly, ever so gently
Those beautiful nipples
I suckled them softly, slowly
For, I wanted to enjoy every moment of my lips on her
breasts.

We drenched in passion
We only knew waves of pleasure, not waves of fear

For the first time in my life, I lost myself…to her, and I felt
free.

Drenched in passion
We felt liberated
We hugged, we kissed, we laughed, we made love.

We stretched our minds,
We stretched our bodies,
We stretched our imagination,
It was so wonderful, so satisfying.

We kissed hard, we kissed soft,
We made love fast, we made love slow,
It was so wonderful, so liberating,
The passion was so drenching.

No words can describe the sheer ecstasy felt when I kissed
her all over.

My mouth suckled her lips, one by one
My lips plunged into her mouth, in search of unexplored
sensations
Her hands, ever so gentle around my hips, now started to
tighten
Her nails pierced, it was painful to my flesh
But I was drowning in passion, complemented by her
panting.

Her hands, inch by inch, was explored by my eagerly
desirous lips

Holding my hand
She guided my fingers to stroke, to plunge for more
sensations
She was delighting in each moment
Her soft belly, her smooth thighs, her voluptuous hips,
They were nectar to my thirsty lips.

Kama Sutra was our guide to our passionate lovemaking.

Every position so intricate,
Everybody part so dexterous,
Loving making was no longer mysterious.

It was rhythmic,
She wanted it slow, she wanted it fast,
She wanted in on the bed, she wanted it on the floor,
She wanted it seating, she wanted it standing.

I followed every wish of hers,
Every touch, every move of mine, she controlled,
And, our lovemaking was all the richer.

It was passion par excellence, beyond my wildest
imagination
I felt so complete, so loved, so wanted, like never before
She drenched me in passion
Passion like never before.

So complete, so sublime, so beautiful, so erotic
It made me beg for more
Passion liberated my soul

My deep-seated fears flowed out of my mind and body, in
whole
In its place, there is now passion
Passion for love, desire, lust, lovemaking, beauty, serenity,
that is she.

Passion is total, so mythical
It made our love-making lyrical
Two souls making love like never-before
I cannot ask for more.

Passion is karma
Her perfect gift to me
To live in peace with myself is to be in love with her.

Drenched in passion,
I realised my existence is not in vain.

Drenched in passion, the flames of our souls came alive
Flame of Love, Flame of Joy, Flame of Tears.

Drenched in love, I could not have asked for a more
fulfilling passion.

Cry My Beloved Mother

Mother is in pain
Our attempts to help looks to be in vain.

When she cries,
Our rivers run dry.

Time infinite, she has always overcome challenges, big and
small
She has given birth to her earthlings, big and small
Tendered them with care and verve for millenniums
Only to see many of them disappear, forever.

She has seen herself transformed, again, and again, and
again
The weather, the oceans, the animal kingdoms
She has seen oceans formed and transformed
Animals appear and disappear.

But as a preamble to her stoic character
Which will be on display for millenniums
She held her heart and mind together and marched on

Much to the amazement of her family members, the other
planets.

Forever the optimist
She soldiered on with stoic and unremitted love
For she knows that if she gives up
Her little Garden of Eden will come to standstill, even cease.

But now, she looks to be in pain, vulnerable, exhausted
She is wondering if her efforts for millions of years have
been in pain
Have her most able children, we humans, driven her insane?

What have we all done to make her so despondent?
Like every child that wants to make her parents proud
We studied hard and worked hard
Experimented and conquered.

The universe, oceans, forests, the animals
You name it, we have done it, we like to boast.

Surely, mother must be proud of us, we ask!
We have studied her colours, her luscious colours
We have unearthed her past secrets
And gave meanings to their oblivion in words and images.
Surely, mother must be proud of us, we ask.

Yet, she cries, inconsolably
She has lost her vivaciousness, her colours, her magic
She looks so tragic
Why?

Yes, we have succeeded beyond our wildest dreams
Those are our dreams and her dreams too.

But mother is horrified
Because, her most blessed children have lost their humanity
The most precious of our emotions.

In our daze of excitement,
We have simply forgotten our fellow earthlings.

Where once earthlings could play in lush gardens of colours
Now, fewer earthlings are alive to see the increasing
desolate lands
Much like the lifeless wind-swept wintry areas in the arctic.

Where once she saw multitude of earthlings all seasons in all
corners of her paradise
Now, mother is reduced to tears when she sees so few of us.

Where once all earthlings can enjoy clear skies and blue seas
Now, we all suffer from pollution on air, land and seas.

Where once formidable predators roamed the forests,
The oceans, and the mountains
Today, they have been decimated, reduced to a sorry state
Where they must hide from us,
Begging for mercy for their continued existence.

Mother cries
And we now know why.

She yearns for all earthlings to live in harmony
And, it can only and must start with us humans
Is it too much to ask of us a little humanity, humility?

It is not just mother is crying
Listen with your heart, and you will hear the cries of all
earthlings.

The abused animals in our backyards
So cruelly mutilated, laughed at and dumped by our fellow
humans
The grey wolves that not only have to rely on their natural
Instincts to survive on a dwindling prey population and
living habitat
But also, on the ability of animal rights proponents
To petition the governments, and against farmers and
hunters.

The majestic tigers, reduced to a pauper state of existence
May not be around for long to arouse the
Imagination of future youths.

The list goes on and on
Is it not in us to think of and appreciate our common
heritage?
Don't we all love our mother enough to nurse her soul
So that all earthlings can share our common heritage, our
mother?

Is it not in our conscience to leave a legacy for our children?
A legacy that will speak volumes of our human dignity

Our ingenuity, our magnanimity, our ability
To live in harmony with Mother Nature.

Forests empty of life
Oceans plundered of live stocks
Air, sea, and land full of toxicity
This is not a legacy anyone can be proud of.

Let us not be so taken in by flashes of success today
Success is for future generations to live for and judge by
Let us not be limited by our definitions of success.

Let us put our hands together to quench our mother's
hunger-pang
A hunger for humility from her most-gifted children, we
humans.

Our mother is crying, and she needs help
And, she needs our help, NOW!
Will you help?

Broken

Broken heart
Broken soul
A life put on hold.

Broken promises
Broken trust
A relationship gone awry.

Broken faith
Broken understanding
Into an abyss, life is sinking.

Broken ideas
Broken leadership
A bleak stewardship.

Broken earth
Broken saviour
A future earth a lot less safe.

Broken confidence
Broken dreams
A cry for help to make meaning.

Broken education
Broken freedom
A future filled with ignorance.

Broken ideals
Broken dreams
Hearts of tears.

Broken families
Broken responsibilities
A future of broken societies.

Broken societies
Broken communities
A society stripped of fabric.

Broken cohesion
Broken mission
A country heading into oblivion.

Broken ownership
Broken fellowship
A country full of brinkmanship.

Broken pieces here and there
Broken pieces every where
A future less perfect for all, beware.

Dreams of a Child

I have many dreams
Simple, sweet, innocent dreams
At least, that is what my friends and I seem to think
Can you listen to our dreams and the reality, please?

We like candies and chocolates
We like to pay marbles, and, hide-and-seek
When it rains, we want to go out and play happily
Home away from home without worries.

Simple, sweet, innocent dreams
That is what we children all think.

But these dreams seem so distant to us
Like so many children in this world
We have many dreams
But life has been cruelling to us.

I am a child labour and only ten years old
Like other child labourers, I work almost everyday
All sweat and no hay
Just tears, in my heart, and, in my mind

Why are we children getting persecuted?
Why must children lose their childhood sense of innocence?

This depressing environment, I have become used
I have lost all sense of time, spatial and temporal
So frigid am I becoming in my heart
That my biggest fear is that my tear wells will soon dry up.

There are so many like me in my neighbourhood
I think there are many more in this world suffering from
such a livelihood
I don't know how to tell in numbers for I have never gone to
school.

This is my destiny, my fate, my mother keeps telling me.

But we children have dreams
Not just to eat and play
But, to grow up and be someone in society.

Can the adults listen to us, please?

I heard there are women lawyers, doctors, musicians
I want to be one of them
I also want to dress well, look beautiful, live happily and
freely
Just like the many women who appear in the television and
newspapers.

Is this too big a dream for adults to handle?
But mother tells me that I am fated to be poor, illiterate, and,
a child bride
Is this true?
How cruel can my parents be?

I am only ten, but I am told I talk like thirty by many adults
But I will not stop talking because I cannot accept my
present fate.

I have seen and suffered so much hardships in my short
lifetime
To know that when people become hungry
Their hearts have no mercy, but only cruelty
But, in my heart, I dream and wish like my true age.

All I am asking for is some tender mercy
Is that too much to ask for in this world?

When I study,
My brothers and sisters will not be starved and stunted of
dreams
Their souls will not be dwarfed by the unremitting struggle
to survive
Waiting to be liberated by death.

When I graduate
I want to start a school to educate all children, especially
girls
Because, we girls are treated worse than animals
I want to change all that.

I want to be a new woman
A woman of independence, with feelings, likes and dislikes
I want to make my own decisions so that I can make my own
paradise.

I don't want to be like my mother.

I want to be a judge
I will make laws so that girls can only marry when they
become adults
Unlike now, where girls as young as ten are married off and
raped by men
Again, and again despite the pain and humiliation to their
tender souls
How sad that parents are complicit to such violence.

There are many like me in this world
We children want our dreams to be the clarion calls of our
universe
But our parents are not listening to us
They only live for today
But we children want to live for the future.

I need your help
We need your help
For, despite our dreams and brave words
We are helpless in this adult world.

In my real world, children are treated as cheap labour and
sex slaves
Years of abuse by monsters have numbed our souls

These monsters lurk everywhere – homes, streets and in the
workplaces.

This is the world many young children like me inhabit
A world where children and abuse cohabit
With no pithy, no mercy from anyone.

We children cling on to each other for support
But though we are exhausted
We want to rise like a phoenix and soar to new heights
We know that there are adults who love children
We know that not all parents are like my parents
Who have no dreams, no heart, no soul!

I am just a child
A child of this world, a child to all of you
A child who wants a better world
And I need your help
We need your help

Will you listen to us?
Will you help us achieve our dreams?
This is my dream…dreams of a child

Farewell

Say farewell to doubts
Doubts caste a long shadow over your abilities.

Say hello to confidence
Confidence nourishes your soul in permanence.

Say farewell to self-pity
It sinks you into an abyss of self-absorption.

Say hello to self-discovery
Discovery reaffirms your duty
Duty to the many.

Say farewell to anger
Anger blocks your mind and heart
It mutates into self-destruction, making you fall apart.

Say hello to tranquillity
It helps to stay focused on the now
It guides you to plan with the spiritual know-how.

Say farewell to hatred
It only makes you a bigot.

Say hello to love
Love for all makes you an angel.

Say farewell to prejudice
Prejudice of colour, race, religion, ethnicity
It divides us, and poisons our shared humanity.

Say hello to diversity
Love and respect for diversity makes us inclusive
That is the best gift from all of us to humanity.

Say farewell to past grievance
For, it only engenders hatred in permanence.

Say hello to forgiveness
It helps us to live with humaneness.

Say farewell to paper chase
It only makes you go in circles, putting your life to waste.

Say hello to real-life experiences
It brings you down-to-earth and stay grounded.

Say farewell to greed
Greed only makes you self-centred, and, hatred breeds.

Say hello to contentment

Contentment opens new opportunities for sharing and
Fulfilment

Say Farewell to everything that destroys our shared
Humanity

Say Hello to virtues that will help us to live tranquillity.

Come to Me

Why won't you come near me, my sweetheart?
For I yearn for the peace that can only be divined by your
gentle touch.

With all the stars of love in this universe wrapped around
your body
Only in you can I find the love that is holy.

Oh, please come near me
With you by my side, I will have peace for eternity.

Your smile exudes love so innocently, so effortlessly
That it will soothe a wounded heart miraculously.

Your laughter is so charming
I want to see it till the day I stop breathing
Eyes so luscious
Lips so vivacious
Hips so curvaceous
You are beauty par excellence,
You are my Venus.

Oh, please come near me
For only you by my side, can I have peace for eternity.

You are graceful so effortlessly
But don't you need a beloved to admire your beauty?
Let it be me, my Venus
Yes, you are my Venus
Such is my obsession with love
That I have given you the status of God.

You are my God
My Goddess of Beauty.

Yes, you are mine
And, mine only.

Oh, please come near me
For only you by my side, can I have peace for eternity.

Failures the Unsung Heroes

In a world of plenty
Success is ubiquity
Unbridled greed has become the new sanity.

Admission of limitations is not seen as honesty
But rather as frailty.

Limitations equal failures, so goes the new mantra
And failures need to be kept afar.

But, humanity feeds on failures
That has always been our history
We need failures to sustain us
Failures keeps us alive.

The sweetness of success is paved with the nectar of failure.

Failures remind us of our limitations
Limitations in talents, limitations of knowledge.

Only when we acknowledge such limitations
Can we look beyond the horizon for opportunities.

Failure liberates us
It empowers us
Failure enforces humility on us.

In humility lies virtuosity.

Often, we place ourselves in the centre of the universe
But failures help to free us from the vanity of selfishness.

The thought that everything starts with us
Everything must end with us
Everything must and only be about us
Nothing is more fool-hardy than this
Failures are the perfect antidote to humanity's vanity.

It brings us down to earth
It makes us realise that we are but part of humanity
That we exist to use our talents to complement one another
To make the world a better place for all of us.

Failures are there to remind us that we are only human
That we need all talents to make things happen
That every action of ours will make an impact on others
That we are but only stewards of this world, not as masters.

So, let us give due credit to failures
It is a path well-trodden by humanity
It makes us more human,
It makes all more accepting of one another
Let us applaud the unsung heroes within us
Let us cherish the wisdom of failures.

Women Are Magic

Magic is to be mesmerised by her eyes, the luscious eyes
The pearl of the Nile.

Magic is to be smiled at by the fullness of her beauty
The beauty where innocence meets virtue
The beauty where I can always plunge into the fullness of
god's love
Where there is no end to the depth of love, a woman's love.

Magic to me is to be cared for, guided by, listened to, by a
woman
My nirvana on earth
No, No, Humanity's nirvana on earth
God's infinite mansion on earth where all men can reach for
Eternity without fear of getting turned away.

Women! How magical they are
And yet, how so mystified we men are
So lost are we of their magic,
That often-times, their fates with us is tragic.

Like the vast oceans of our world
Women are infinite sources of wisdom in all corners of our
universe.

When you want a taste of the sweet touch of the fullness of
the universe
Go to a woman
There, you will feel the gentle streams of love flowing
beneath your feet.

Magic will be our world
When every man listens to women, love them, respect them,
accept them
Women are souls so full of love, tender love
They nourish us, body and soul.

With women by your side
You can never grow up spiritually stunted and starved
Instead, you will grow up to love everyone
Not just fellow humans, but so too the natural world, and the
universe.

Because only a woman's love, her gentle touch, her milk can
Give you the source of wisdom to understand the inter-
connectedness of our universe
And, the importance of nourishing all of them with tender
care.

There is a reason why we call our earth as our mother
You see, earth does not survive on its own

Men know this, but they can only explain with scientific
discoveries
But only women know the mysteries, the inter-
connectedness,
The pain, and, the labour of love of mother earth.

Women are the sustenance of our lives
Without she, no pearls of wisdom can be planted in any
child
No scientific wonders can replace this act
No matter how hard we may all try to alter the fact.

Magic is the innate ability of women to raise warriors,
thinkers,
Lovers, and philosophers
For, only she can ever implant in the of-springs of her womb
The seeds of wisdom.

Is it not important than for all us to embrace women?
To respect them, not exploit their flesh,
To love them, not turn them into sex slaves,
To nurture them, not turn them into child labour.

If we men can worship mother earth,
Why can't we embrace women?
God's unique gift to the universe,
Her personification on earth.

To me, God is a woman
For only a woman can understand the mystics of a childbirth
And, the birth of our universe.

If we believe in a God, a Creator,
Then, why on earth are we abusing her?

Embrace them, love them, respect them
For they are embodiment of all that is unique to our earth
For our existence, for our soul, for our eternity.

Without women, we will all turn into victims of poverty
Poverty of love
Poverty of compassion.

Without women, the earth will roll through a void
Void in all souls
Souls of the outer world, souls of the oceans,
Souls of the skies, and, souls of the earth surface.

Without women, hungry clouds will swag on the deep,
Looking for love in the vastness of our sky,
Only to turn away empty-handed with tears,
Tears of dejection that will flood our souls with sadness.

Without women, life will be an unceasing struggle for
meaning,
Where we can only sleep, but not dream.

Without women, how can the world be spellbound?
Without women, who can understand our emotions, our
thoughts?

Without women, our spirituality, our emotions will fall into
silence

They will become the silent wind
And like the silent wind,
We can only feel it, not touch it, feel it, not embrace it.

Is this the kind world we all want to live without women?
Let us cherish our magic…WOMEN of this world.

Prostitution

Another day
Another dollar
A life forever at bay
A life without a future.

A bleak life I live
A better life, I have longed ceased to believe.

Prostitution is my profession
I was forced into it, despite my protestation.

I work in a strange land
To survive, I had to adapt to my economic hinterland
The hinterland that has put all my dreams and hopes to a
dead-end.

I was promised riches
To my self-worth, there will be no glitches
Or so, I was made to believe by the witches.

Yes!
Those conniving witches are real bitches

Once in the new land, I was herded like cattle
Not just me, but, many others.

We cried, we screamed, but in vain
Strange!
We all spoke different languages, but our sentiments were
the same.

To control us, we were forced to witness each other's
humiliation
Men taking turns to rape each woman
Blood everywhere, Tears everywhere, Fears everywhere
But help was nowhere.

Our gender became our liability
We were robbed of our virginity
We were stripped of our dignity
Literally, figuratively.

These men now owned us
Literally, figuratively
Our lives were dependent on their fancies.

We became possessions
Flesh without senses
Smile without happiness
And, souls of emptiness.

Our profession is harlotry
For married women, such actions constitute adultery
But for people like me, society only dishes out bigotry

Every day, seven days a week, we work
We dress up with no pleasure
Our bodies, our souls have lost their emotions.

Men of different sizes, colours, odour make love
No, no, it is not love
They penetrate me
They humiliate me
I have long lost all my emotions for love making.

I move according to their wishes
My blank eyes stare into empty spaces
And, I repeat this routine every day till the midnight hour
ceases.

I look at myself in the mirror, I only see a dead person
Living without passion, dreams, acceptance
Not just me, every woman like me is a walking corpse
We are alive, but only in name
Feeling death in our souls, we are all the same.

We have no relief
No relief from abuses
No relief from our own hapless suffocating silence.

I have not seen my parents, my siblings, my neighbours for
years
For their well-being, I am always full of fears.

Many a time, we have tried to run away
But, once caught, we are mutilated, and locked away
Our hopes of freedom have simply melted away.

There are girls as young as fifteen
I am a veteran in this trade at nineteen.

Why are people so cruel?
I was tricked by women into this trade
Don't they have sisters, mothers, and daughters?
We are treated as slaves by men
Don't they have sisters, wives, daughters, and mothers?

Where have all their humanity gone?
Will we all despair someday, when we are no longer wanted,
accepted?
Like I am, and forever doomed to be?

Do I need to live such a life? I ask myself
But I honestly have no answers.

I have simply turned into a living corpse, a walking corpse
Flesh without feelings, smile without warmth.

I am numb, emotionally numb
I have long stopped dreaming, thinking, becoming
intellectually dumb
Yes, blood flows in my vein
But they are maimed.

I have simply turned into a living corpse, a walking corpse
Flesh without feelings, smile without warmth.

Is there no end to bigotry?
Is there no end to society's hypocrisy?
Is there no end to our agony?
Please tell me.

If Only

If only I had smiled
You will be still alive
Such a tender soul you were, I did not know.

No, no, no more lies.

I know, I know
I was a monster in person, then I did not know.

Now, I know, I know
But it is all too late.

If only I had hugged, you will be still alive
Alive with cheers
Laughter and tears
Most of all, your loved ones will all smile.

How cruel of me to make you die
Die of fateful love
Die of loveless love.

No more lies, no more lies
I did not return your love
I only thought of myself
You just became a footnote.

I made love to you with but with no love in my heart
I embraced you but with emotions depart.

I thought you will never know
But know you did
You cried, but I laughed
The laughter of sins, the laughter of cynicism.

Now, now…
Now, I am all alone
All lonely in my death bed.

I now long for someone to touch me
Someone to talk to me
But there is no one.

You were the only one who came closest to me
Yet, I did not embrace it unconditionally.

You were the only one who cared for me
Yet, I did not appreciate it.

You were the only soul willing to give me a chance
But I blew it.

Now, I want you
But I can't reach you
Now, I want to embrace you
But I can't touch you.

If only, if only, I had loved you when it mattered
If only…

Gateway to Heaven

Your nose ring …the perfect ornament
To grace earth's most perfect beauty ever to be.

It smiles when your heart expresses love in a way that only
you can
And it blushes when your beauty is admired to no end.

Women become mesmerised by its simple beauty
Men turn into statues by its magic words…God's very own
poetry.

It melts your words into honey
And, it is music to your voice that is forever heavenly.

It is the gateway to my heaven that is your heart
A heart like no other I had seen, felt, or loved
A heart that is the kingdom of eternal grace, charm and
beauty
The heaven that will always keep my soul eternally happy.

But, am I dreaming? It cannot be…It must not be
For, if it is a dream, I will shrink and never be
Because I am spellbound by its sheer elegance forever be.

The Gateway to Heaven…Heaven's gift to earth
Your ring…the eternal flame of beauty…it will always be…

My Sweet Angel

O My Sweet Angel!
Where are you?
Where have you been?
I miss you so much
Your laughter, your smile, your everything.

The eyes of yours
Always alive, laughing together and smiling at each other
Truly a poet's utopia, god's gift to me.

Your face, the luminous face,
That is eternally beautiful to me,
As the sunrise is to mother earth's continued existence to be.

Your lips, magical lips,
That turns red ruby when you blush
God's perfect complement to my soul's longing for its other
half.

I miss touching your hair
The impossibly coiffed hair
In which my soul is eternally at peace and will not despair

But my sweet angel, where are you? Where have you been?
I miss you so much you know.

You caressed me when I was down
You breasted me close to your heart when I was in tears
You gave me unremitted love even when I was angry with
you
You, you…the saint in my imperfect life.

Maybe, you left me because humanity left me
I was never there for you when you needed me, I now realise
How I wish that my past life I can revive and revise.

I took your love unconditionally
Yet, returned it sparingly
I took your calming touch, kiss, and embrace whole-
heartedly
Yet, never embraced you genuinely
How cruel I have been, I now realise.

You were more than a partner to me
You loved me more than anyone did in my life
You set my life on redemption,
When all others poured resentment.

You were my saint, my goddess of love.

Soulless man can rule the world with crude power
But it is the unconditional embrace of a woman that adds
Meaning to our lives forever.

I now realise all these
But like countless men,
I too never learned to appreciate a woman's love to no end.

You left my life long ago
You left a life turned imperfect by me.

You left me to touch God's face
And, I know she will embrace you unconditionally
And give you the love I denied you.

I despair now of my stupidity
What use now for a more perfect life for me
For, without you, it will never be.

I want to be with you and not anyone anew
You understood me like no one else
How foolish of me to never embrace the world given to me
by you.

I miss you so much, you know!
I want to be with you, only I now know.

When I finally close my eyes,
And, my soul takes leave of this temporal existence
I want to make up to you, each day, every day.

Forgive me for my sins, I implore you
I now repent and long to be with you.
Will you ever embrace me when I longingly wait to see
You at the gates of heaven, my sweet angel?

Himalayan Mystique

Land of mystique
Land of esoteric
Land of mountains clothed in midst.

Hiding behind the midst
Endless luster I will not want to miss.

Oh Himalaya, Himalaya
You banish all my fears of yesteryears.

A lonely soul, I thought I am
Until you lid my heart with your charm of lamp.

Oh Himalaya, Himalaya
You banish all my fears of yesteryears
I was a wondering soulless nomad yesterday
Until you lid my heart with hopes of rays.

Rays of colours
Rays of lovers
Hopelessly in love with you, my heart is bedevilled.

Once my mood of sadness was inexhaustible
Trying to find solace I once thought was impossible.

No more, no more
When I see you, I want you more!

Oh Himalaya, Himalaya
You banish all my fears of yesteryears.

I want to reach for the mountain atop the sky
To be with you, alone
Heart to heart.

Oh, don't move away from my memory
For, I won't go away from your heart.

I want you to be my soul's river stream
Always there to be by my side.

Let us not be apart
For if we do, I fear our souls will depart.

My wondering was anti-dharma
You, the nectar of my soul, is dharma.

With you, I can no longer mask my ego
For you have effortlessly exposed my soul that was in limbo.

Do not go away from me
For I promise that I will be a lifelong messenger of your love
As long you are with me.

My Lonely Dove

My lovely dove, Brume
How are you today?

You look unsettled today. Why?
The lively curved moon crescent lips of yours is dour. Why?
Tell me, for your sadness is also mine
In spirit and in mind.

You whom I worship with fondness
For helping me rise above my own little world
To see the bigger universe with peace and love
How can I stay with serenity when my angel looks so sad?

Where there is tumult in my life and in this universe,
You always rise above
Above me and so many others, like a phoenix, full of life,
To bring to many wounded a spirit of bright.

Won't you share your gloom with me?

With you as my guide,
I have learned to feed on love
And give my love to others in need.

Is it not time for me to share your sorrows?

Like doves who visit desolate souls
To share their dews of love and peace,
You have always shared your love
No matter where, no matter who.

Now, you are sad
And, your tears have made my heart wet.

Your affection is unique
You speak up, not just for the poor, the ignorant, and, the downtrodden
But also, for the silent
For the animals, skies and oceans
This is affection par excellence.

Your fluttering eyes
Your graceful walk
Your effervescent smile
They will always make this world a better place to be.

You give love and peace to me, ALWAYS
You are my faithful friend, ALWAYS
You are there for me, ALWAYS.

And yet, today, you are sad. Why?
Won't you share your sorrows with us, Brume?

I wait for you daily
Just like tired souls waiting for the doves to share peace and
love
And, you have never failed me with your love and affection,
every day.

How can a sweet angel like you be sad?

You are my symbol of love and peace
You epitomise the best of this world
Beauty, grace, love, and, peace.

Please don't be lonely.

If you become lonely,
My world will be empty
In an uncertain world, the world will miss an angel of mercy.

I need you
The world needs you
Don't be lonely, Brume
Come to me, come to us and be happy as ever be
For a better world to be.

Sea of Love

Sea of Love, I always long for
And, she returns my yearning, like never before.

No matter the seasons
No matter the tides
No matter the feelings
She always seems to have me in her sight.

She smiles
She cries
In tandem with all my emotional plight.

She comes by many names
Each so exquisite, each with its own fame.

The Red Sea
The Black Sea
She is colour spectacular for all to see.

The South China Sea
The Arabian Sea
She even speaks of nationalities

For millenniums, life has revolved around her vastness
Food for survival
Scenes of epic battles
Mover in search of new lands
Inspiration for romance.

When the skies glow,
She waxes lyrical
When the winds blow,
She sways rhythmical.

Sea of Love
So vast, So mysterious
So unpredictable
Yet, so reliable.

Feelings of love,
Feeling of fear,
Feelings of seduction,
Feelings of apprehension,
I am always in trepidation.

With you, the world is so complete
Beauty and romance
Danger and courage
You epitomise everything, sea of love
How can I think of a world without you?

Sea of Love…You are my love beyond measure

My Oracle

In years pass, all I ever wanted to see was me
For, no one saw any meaning in me.

And so, I lived in a room full of mirrors
So that wherever I turned to, I saw me, only myself
And nothing else.

It was an existence of solitude, depravity
But it was the only way to escape human's monstrosity
A monstrosity of giggles and hostility.

Then in a serendipitous moment, you came into my life
And, I have never looked back
It was the day my oracle arrived
And, not a day has since passed when I did not listen to your
words
Words coming straight from the deity, how can they be
wrong?

Where there were only dusty plains in my environs
Now, I see flooded plains, full of life, love and romance

Where there was once a surfeit of hatred
Now every day, every moment, I am inundated with love
So strong that the downpour continues well-nigh into the
mornings.

Reality is cruel
But in you, it has also blessed me with surprise.

Once I was drowning in the surrounding tempestuous seas,
Peopled by the damning voices of fellow humans
Now, I float in a sea of oasis
It is now my universe of *Felix* – Happy Universe

Where I once fell instantly to the bottom of the ranks of
humanity
You now engage me in an outrageous display of thespians of
vanity
And how glad I am that my oracle had arrived
With my oracle by my side, I live in paradise.

With you by me,
I race across the breath of the savannah of love, pure and
simple
And, perform an elaborate pantomime of unalloyed altruism
An altruism of love, pure and simple.

The softness of your expression says a thousand words
It helps every picture of yours tell a story
It helps me to be me, love myself, accept myself.

You ooze a sexuality that is quixotic, so outside of this
world
And yet, you are so sure-footed to let me with you
It charms me to no end
And, I hope it never ends.

Where once my life was filled with arid air
Now, it is scented with perfume, in your presence.

Once my universe was nothing more than a black hole,
A labyrinth to stare at with despair
Now, it is an everglade of love in your cosmic presence.

A cosmic of love
A cosmic of childlike innocence
A cosmic of an angel's sense of beauty.

An air of humour and levity has come into my life
And my life now is paradise, now and forever
You are my oracle, now and forever.

Full Moon

Selene, Goddess of the Moon
Strong and beautiful
Yet, gentle and graceful
You are the perfect beauty, my heart swoons.

Crisscrossed the globe, I did,
In search of my perfect soulmate
But you did not appear,
And I waited, and waited, till you appeared.

You are my moon, my full moon
You swim so gracefully in the oceans of the sky
So graceful that I am oblivious to my life moments going by.

You are my moon, my full moon
A soul mate for my insatiable lust
A dream beauty that for my life will lasts
And, to my void life, you add the missing ballast.

You are my moon, my full moon
You appear all the time, not once in a blue moon
You are the full moon my heart swoons

To many, a full moon is hard to come by
But to me, a full moon appears always, side by side
You are the full moon I live with, and live by
My full moon, full of grace and charm, I will never bid
goodbye.

Mere mortals we all are, but not you, Selene.

Like all others, I am just a tiny thread in this universe's life
But you, you are the fabric that holds me alive.

Your delicate tracery is the work of God
For, how else, can I fathom your perfect beauty.

Perfection of beauty
Beauty of perfection.

You are the full moon in my life
Without your presence, I will die.

Just as the moon is vital for life's existence
My soul will only be blissful upon your benediction.

In you, I see the past, the present, and, the future.

Your presence tells me of the evolution of beauty
Your presence tells me of life's beautiful complexity
Your presence shows me the secrets of the future symmetry
A future symmetry of perfect beauty and grace, life and
death.
My full moon, Selene, how lucky am I!

March of the Follies

"Power corrupts
And absolute power corrupts absolutely,"
So said Lord Acton.

How true for eternity!

"Evil springs from unchecked goodness,"
So said Reinhold Neibuhr.

How true of humanity!

Yes, we never learn from history
Instead, we march on like follies.

Follies, I dare say
For, from time immemorial
Humanities' hymn has been that successive generations will
be different
From their predecessors and neighbours.

But nothing changes in power relations
And deep in our heart, we all know why

And yet, we keep trying only to end up marching as follies,
Again, and again.

Why?

Because, even when we all know these to be acts of delusion
We all partake in them in acts of desperation.

Why?

Because we have leaders who promise us utopia
Only for all of us to fall flat on our dreams of euphoria.

The economy crawls
The credit ratings fall.

Politicians will appear before us in new garments
Promising to turn our miserable lives around with their
economic dogmas.

Religious leaders will lead us on prayers
Promising heaven upon earth, if all of us follow these
soothsayers.

Why?

History is replete of such follies
Great leaders have succumbed to the delusion of hubris
Napoleon, MacArthur, Caesar.
But we never learn from history
Instead, we continue to choose ignorance

We ignore the essence and limits of humanity
And instead, embrace bigotry

Bigotry!

Yes, I am talking about the bigotry of power.

You can see the results all around you
This bigotry devours our environment.

This bigotry devours our neighbours
It devours neighbouring countries.

This bigotry robs all of us of dignity
It devours our natural assets.

It devours our essence of humanity.

Yet, we continue to live in our delusion
And carry on the march as follies.

Why?

Because, like our leaders, we too have our dreams
Like them, our dreams are all temporal, not spatial.

Because we have mastered science
We see ourselves as masters, not as stewards of this universe

We render all others voiceless
The animals, the plants, the sea, the birds, our neighbours

Everyone, except us, we individuals.
They are to be conquered, subjugated
All through the seasons, generations after generations to
serve our needs
And, we never complain
Because we can never feel their pain.

But, when pain comes to us, we plead for help
Seemingly oblivious to our complicity in the scheme of
things.

Like our leaders, we too yearn for a grandiose history
Hoping to be part of a self-created glorious chapter of
humanity.

How folly are we!
Don't we all know the price we have to pay to be?

We are all delusional, follies
Good times and bad times
We all fall for grandiose schemes as history has proven
many a times.

Scientific marvels, political cohesion, subtle subjugation
We humans have internalised and rationalised the logic of
folly.

Why?

Because, we all want short-term solutions to the long-term
ills

Self-inflicted ills that comes from bigotry, ignorance and
greed.

We are all follies
And, we will continue to march as follies.

Tears I Miss You

Tears!
Expressions of happiness
Expressions of sadness
Lovely, but contradictory.

Tears!
Tears of losing
Tears of winning
Lovely, but contradictory.

Tears!
We shed tears when we unite in love of hearts
We shed tears when love falls apart
Sad, and contradictory.

Tears!
Tears of sincerity
Tears of duplicity
Sad, and, contradictory.

Tears!
A beautiful gift to express the best and worst of humanity

They speak a thousand words in their spontaneity
They transcend all boundaries of geography.

But I have no tears
I shed no tears on my father's death
He, who loved me so much
Yet, I shed no tears for him, even when I was alone.

I shed no tears for my lovely sisters
My sisters who still love me despite my imperfection
They cried because of my insensitive scolding
Yet, not once did I own up, or, shed tears.

I shed no tears for my loving mother
A strong-willed woman who toiled for me
She cried when I verbally abused her for selfish reasons
Yet, I shed no tears.

My wife and daughter
They cry when I scold them
Yet, not once, have I ever shed tears for them.

Tears are for weaklings, I learned when young
When I cried in pain, I was bullied
When I cried, I was not pitied.

"Men must never cry," I firmly believed.

Now, I am much older, and, wiser
Try as I may, I am not able to shed tears

My heart has hardened
I am beyond redemption.

Now, when I see men cry, I feel jealous
Without tears, I fear I will be oblivious.

Win or lose, joy or sorrow
I have never shed tears.

I learnt not to shed tears when I was little
For, to shed tears is to make my heart brittle.

Once, it was a badge of honour
Now, I realise it has made me a sinner.

Then, I was prone to wishful thinking
When I was a man of limited insights and meaning.

Now, I am wiser
But I am also a loser.

Loser I am because, no matter how much I repent,
I am unable to persuade my tear wells that resent
Yes, they resent my pleas to cry.

I am unable to cry when I say sorry to my wife
I am unable to cry when I seek my mother's forgiveness
I am unable to cry with my little daughter when she cries
because of me.
My loved ones have shed so much tears for me, because of
me

They cried when I finally graduated
They had faith in me when no one else did
They cried when I hurt them
Yet, not once have I shared in their tears of joy, hurt, or,
sorrow.

Now, I fear
I fear of losing them
There is so much to tell them
But without tears, who is going to believe me.

The Holy Grail to my humanity is in my tears
Tears must be God's gift to humanity
Yet, I refused to believe in her gift because of my stupidity.

There is so much tears I want to shed
Tears of happiness, tears of asking forgiveness, tears of
guilt, tears of love.

Yet, my old fear haunts me.

What if they start thinking I am weak?
Where has the strongman gone?

Or, is it my delusion?
My delusion of being a strong man?
A strong man, but, with no heart, no feelings, no tears?
I am confused and lost for answers.

I want my tears
I want my tears back now

They can help me regain my humanity, give answers to my
questions.

Tears, please come back
Tears, please forgive me
Please come back to add sincerity to my newfound
humanity.

Tears…I miss you

Silence of Death

Silence is such a magic, many say,
Silence to meditate,
Silence to concentrate,
Silence to tell us that everything is OK.

But silence also has a darker side.

When we don't speak up for what is right,
It is not silence of wisdom,
Rather, it is silence of death.

When you refuse to stop evil deeds by anyone, anywhere,
It means silence of death.

Silence can mean death, by choice
A choice when we decide to remain silent.

I am only one
But, when I decide to remain silent to violence just because I
am only one,
I am choosing death with my silence.

This death can be physical
It can also be emotional
It can be spiritual.

When we decide not to speak for the downtrodden,
We are choosing to condemn them to death
With our silence and ignorance.

When we choose to ignore unjust leaders,
We are choosing death by silence.

Death to our conscience
Death to truth
Death to equity
Death to justice
Death to humanity.

This death will not stop with us
They will continue into our children's generation
Not exactly a manna from heaven.

When we remain silent to the untold cruelty done to animals,
We are leaving a legacy of death with our silence.

When we remain silent to the damage being done to our
climate,
We are bequeathing a legacy of suffocating death with our
silence.

When we remain silent to child labour, child soldier,
We are leaving a legacy of stunted growth to our children

When we actively engage in denying other people their fair
wages,
We are robbing them and future generations of human
dignity
A result of our complicity
Complicity by our silence.

When we remain silent to violence committed against
women and children,
We are causing death with our silence
Silence that eats into our moral fabric
Silence that does untold physical and emotional harm to
millions
Millions of women and children.

This is silence of death.

But we can choose to be different
Even if you are only one, you are still one
You may not be able to do everything, but you can do
something
And, if each one of us break the taboo of silence and step
forward,
We can make a difference to all our lives.

Say no to the silence of death today.

Free at Last

Yesterday, my life was a blight
Blight to my dignity
Blight to humanity.

I saw no light for the rest of eternity
How can this be?

I cried in shame,
Looking for answers, but, in vain.

I never went to school as I was born a girl
"An inferior creature to boys," murmurs of many a man I
heard
It hurt, and still hurts
I only stayed at home, and, never had to face life's
wherewithal.

Cloistered, I could only talk to my mother
My mother dedicated her whole life to her family
Yet, deep beneath, she was devoid of any happiness.

She could not read, or, write.
Like me, she only stayed at home to look after domestic
duties
Like me, she was also considered an inferior creature
But what a loving mother she was to all of us
Always there to console us despite all her physical and
emotional frailties
She died a sad death, in my arms, in her home, but with no
one around.

Her death haunted me to no end
Will my own life be like hers, I worried to no end!

The answer came, a rude awakening for me
My father decided to get me married, at age fifteen
My husband to be was old enough to be my father.

My father decided, and that sealed my faith
Married and shipped off to a distant land in Singapore
I had no choice because that was my culture
I became a mother two years later.

Sweet seventeen to many teens
But to a teenage mother like me, life was beginning to be
mean.

Life was hard, but we got by
I was in a land of strangers, who spoke strange languages
I was totally not prepared for this
I cried in vain, but no answers came
Reality was, and, will forever be cruel.

But strangely, it can also spring surprises
Like my mother, I also had to stay at home
Her life and death haunted me
But it also motivated me
I was motivated to be what my mother was never given a
chance to be.

Before long, I too joined the blue-collar workforce
My first step to move away from my mother's fate.

We raised four children
And, not one of my three girls ever married in their teens
No! That is not their fate, and, will never be a fate, I vowed
to my myself.

I made sure my three daughters graduated and were
gainfully employed
I made sure my only son respected women as valued
partners.

My mother would have been proud of me.

I pushed on with an unshakable faith in my womanhood
If women can shoulder life's most beautiful gift of giving
life and caring
Then, we can also aspire beyond the confines of our homes.

My mother must be smiling from heaven
My father must be spinning in his grave.

In all this, I also had a quiet and loving ally, my husband
In a strange land, he too realised old and useless customs
need to die.

Today, absence of my adult children gives me a miss
My husband had also departed this world, and him, I miss
Today, I cried once more
Not tears of shame, but tears of joy
My mother had no education, no liberty
But, not me.

My mother still motivates me from heaven
I looked at myself and asked, what is missing?
And then, it dawned! Education
Yes, education!

And, once again, I started discovering myself anew
With education, I can be free of boredom
With education, I can be free of ignorance
With education, I can be free of humiliation.

With education, I can be what my mother was never given a
chance to be.

I started learning alphabets and numbers
My enthusiasm was the source of endless laughter for my
grandchildren
But their innocent laughter and teaching encouraged me
Baby steps alright, but a giant leap in my life.

My mother cried in my dreams
She is proud of me, I confessed of my dreams to my
daughters
We all cried, including my grandchildren.

Now, I am confident of going to another country on my own
My mother could not even go to the village theatre on her
own.

Now, I can confidently travel and speak to strangers
My mother was not even allowed to speak to her neighbours.

Seven decades on, I am a woman standing tall with dignity
I am someone what my father never meant me to be
I am proud of myself to be free
I am free because I chose to be.

We all can be free in our own lives
No matter where or when, freedom starts with faith in
oneself
With faith, dignity, humility, and, confidence, we all can be
free
Be free like me and many other women and discover
yourself.

Be Free for a better humanity.

The End